THE
OVERCOMERS

THE
OVERCOMERS

GEORGE E. VANDEMAN
MARK FINLEY

Pacific Press Publishing Association
Boise, Idaho
Oshawa, Ontario, Canada

Edited by Jerry D. Thomas
Designed by Tim Larson
Typeset in 10/12 Century Schoolbook

Bible quotations are from the New King James Version
unless otherwise indicated.

The author assumes full responsibility for the accuracy of
all facts and quotations cited in this book.

Library of Congress Cataloging-in-Publication Data:

Vandeman, George E.
    The overcomers / George E. Vandeman, Mark Finley.
        p.   cm.
    ISBN 0-8163-1083-1
    1. Suffering—Religious aspects—Christianity. 2. Con-
solation. 3. Seventh-Day Adventists—Membership. 4. Adventists—Membership.
I. Finley, Mark, 1945-   . II. Title.
BV4909.V36   1992
248.8'6—dc20   91-37998
                                                    CIP

92 93 94 95 96 · 5 4 3 2 1

Contents

Chapter 1

Overcoming an Alcoholic Environment

Ten million Americans are alcoholics, tragic statistics tell us. And that would be sad enough if theirs were the only lives that were ruined. But families suffer too. Spouses are abused, neglected, and lied to. Children are cheated of life's basic necessities—above all a tender, loving parent.

Did you know that one out of every three Americans is a close family member of an alcoholic? Much effort and concern goes into helping the drinkers themselves, and for this we thank God. But what about help for their loved ones, help for the victims of an alcoholic environment?

Many aren't even aware they are living with an alcoholic. Drinkers don't have to wallow in the gutters of skid row to qualify as alcoholics. They might be attractive, articulate, successful professionals—attorneys, physicians, executives, even pastors, priests, and rabbis. What they have in common with down-and-outers on the streets is that their drinking is out of control.

Now, any alcoholic consumption can be dangerous— we all know that even a few drinks can cause death on the highways or loosen one's moral restraints on a night of temptation. But alcoholics have a special problem. They no longer drink merely because they are enjoying it—they simply can't make themselves stop.

Once, they could have a glass of wine on holidays or at dinner and maybe a bottle of beer at a ballgame. Then they began drinking more frequently, perhaps seeking escape from the pain of a crisis or relief from the stress of daily living. Gradually the deadly addiction developed. All too suddenly they became helpless alcoholics, having crossed the line between drinking by choice and drinking by necessity.

Alcoholics are usually dishonest with themselves and with others. They convince themselves that there is no problem, that they can stop drinking anytime they please. They also become masters of manipulating others in order to maintain their habit and still function in their environment.

Unfortunately, families of alcoholics usually help them live their lie by sharing their denial of reality. Psychologists call this "enabling" or "facilitating" the addiction. In the book *Love Is a Choice: Recovery for Codependent Relationships*, we find the story of Claudia Black, a pioneer researcher in this area.

Claudia "was quite young—three, perhaps—when she awoke one morning to see her drunken father sprawled unconscious in the front yard. Terrified, she ran to her mother. 'Mommy! Daddy is lying out there! Something's wrong!'

"Calmly her mother replied, 'No, dear, nothing's wrong. Daddy is camping.'

"Claudia clearly remembers nodding at that very tender age and agreeing, 'Daddy is camping.' Thus as a tiny girl she learned to see a terrifying piece of reality, deny its reality, turn it upside down and say, 'No, things are not as painful and frightening as they seem. It's really okay somehow.'"

Daddy is camping?! Why this compulsion to deny such an obvious reality as alcoholism? Well, for one thing, denying the addiction helps everyone maintain some sense of normalcy and stability. Deluding themselves that everything is OK also relieves them from the responsibility to confront a growing threat to their home. And besides, who wants the whole neighborhood to know that there's an addict in the family? That would be embarrassing.

So everyone pretends nothing is wrong. The family goes on with business as usual while Daddy goes "camping."

Enablers have three unwritten rules that let them live their lie and avoid dealing with a loved one's addiction: (1) don't talk; (2) don't trust; (3) don't feel. Don't talk about the problem; don't trust anyone for help; don't deal with your own feelings of shame, anger, fear, and desperation. What a sad way to live! But that's exactly how millions survive the presence of alcoholism in the family circle.

Well, how do you break loose of bondage to an alcoholic environment? The first step is to stop denying reality. Daddy isn't camping—he has a terrible problem that is ruining his own life and devastating the family. Daddy needs help, and he needs it now!

I think of the experience of a man I'll call John. His co-workers noticed that he drank a lot when they had lunch with their clients. John's performance was obviously affected, but nobody made any real efforts to help him. His wife, Brenda, knew he often stopped at a tavern on his way home. When she complained, he vigorously denied being a problem drinker. And so Brenda, unable to persuade John to reform his ways, gave up and cooperated with his alcoholic habits.

When John was too drunk to keep a dinner appointment, Brenda would lie and tell their friends he had to work late. She brushed aside her children's questions and made them go to bed before their father staggered in the door. Frequently she would pour his vodka down the drain, even though she knew he would only go down to the liquor store and buy another bottle. Beyond scolding him now and then for drinking too much, she did nothing to help with his alcoholism.

Well, what could she do?

The first thing Brenda could do to help John was to get help for herself. The stress of living with an alcoholic had made her a bundle of raw nerves. All the rage and resentment she tried to repress seethed within her soul. Her sense of self-worth had plummeted after years of John's shameful behavior—behavior that he managed to make *her* feel guilty about. Brenda was an emotional and spiritual wreck. Before helping John, she had to come to terms with her own problems.

Brenda found the help she needed at Al-Anon, a non-profit self-help organization for loved ones of alcoholics. Al-Anon has an effective program of peer counseling, where people who are learning to overcome an alcoholic environment share their advice and their testimonies of success—and failure. There's a lot of solid emotional support at Al-Anon meetings, the kind that encourages family members of alcoholics to take positive action rather than just feel sorry for themselves.

At Al-Anon, Brenda learned not to nag, yell, beg, or embarrass her husband about his drinking. Such methods never worked, anyway. She also stopped helping him lie about his drunken absences and quit bailing him out after his bouts of irresponsible behavior. She began practicing tough love—giving John the support every husband needs without letting him manipulate her.

Although Al-Anon isn't geared to any religious persuasion, dependence upon God forms a vital element in the program. Brenda met some Christian women there who invited her to their own weekly prayer group. That's where she finally discovered what she needed more than anything else—a saving relationship with Jesus Christ.

Brenda had unconsciously made John the lord of her life by centering all her hopes and dreams in him. She depended upon him for emotional support, only to be devastated every time he broke his feeble promises. She learned to depend more upon the promises of God's Word. She especially came to appreciate the Psalms. One of her favorites is Psalm 62:5-7:

"Find rest, O my soul, in God alone; my hope comes from him. He alone is my rock and my salvation; he is my fortress, I will not be shaken. My salvation and my honor depend on God; he is my mighty rock, my refuge" (NIV).

It's nice to have the emotional support of a loving spouse, but our ultimate hope must be in God alone. No human being can provide that solid-rock foundation for our lives. Brenda finally accepted Jesus as the friend who never fails. He became the central focus of her life. She formed the habit of rising early every morning for personal Bible study and prayer. There she found the strength to survive and to thrive amid the difficult circumstances of an alcoholic environment.

When we unite our will with God's strength, we can do all things through Christ. Brenda's new faith in God brought wonderful healing to her damaged emotions. At last she felt prepared to help John. She employed a radical strategy often recommended by counselors as the only hope of breaking through the wall of denial behind which alcoholics hide their addiction. Here's how it works.

A meeting is arranged involving all the important people in the alcoholic's life—spouse, children, parents, fellow workers and supervisor, best friends, and the pastor. Without giving advance notice to the alcoholic, all of them meet at an appointed time and place for a loving but forceful confrontation. The meeting must be chaired by someone trained and experienced. One by one around the circle, group members explain how the alcoholic has been hurting them, as well as himself. Nobody condemns the one they are trying to help, but the group refuses to be manipulated or lied to.

During such an encounter, the spouse might find it necessary to threaten a separation in the marriage unless the alcoholic agrees to get help. The work supervisor might make continued employment contingent upon cooperation. On the positive side, both spouse and employer, along with everyone present, offer wholehearted support and affirmation if the alcoholic decides to confront reality.

Naturally, such a meeting is quite painful and emotional. Sometimes the alcoholic gets angry and stalks out. Usually, though, he or she will break down and agree to enter a treatment program. A specific pledge is secured as to what will be done to get help, and that it will happen immediately.

Obviously, this crisis-encounter session must be delicately planned and orchestrated. Especially important is the leadership of someone who is trained and experienced. The people at Al-Anon are well equipped to assist in setting up a tough-love confrontation to rescue an alcoholic loved one. You can locate your local chapter of Al-Anon in the phone book, along with Alateen, a support group for teenagers of alcoholics. If you have any trouble locating either Al-Anon or Alateen, contact Alcoholics Anonymous, or AA. That organization is everywhere in North America, and they will be able to help you.

Well, I'm happy to report that John's crisis intervention turned out well, and he is responding to counseling. But you may be wondering, Was it wrong for Brenda to threaten her husband with separation if he didn't get help for his alcoholism?

You understand, first of all, that we aren't discussing divorce. The Bible does give permission for divorce in situations involving sexual unfaithfulness—although even then the marriage can often be rescued. In other cases, such as with an alcoholic who refuses to get help, the loneliness of separation can be a positive influence in reforming behavior. Time alone to think can be just the medicine needed to convince the alcoholic that he or she cannot continue destroying the family. Remember, the goal of such a separation is to ultimately preserve the family unit.

Now, one final word about John. He is determined to be a responsible husband and father, even though he's made many mistakes along the way. Brenda has learned to forgive all the pain he has caused the family—not because he deserves mercy, but because God accepts all repenting sinners despite their many shortcomings.

This raises important questions: Is alcoholism a sin or merely a disease? Could it be *both* a sin and a disease? No doubt many have a genetic weakness for alcoholism—but all of us suffer from compulsions and predispositions to sin in one way or another. And whenever we indulge these weaknesses, we must face the consequences.

Consider this. It might seem compassionate to tell our loved ones they are helpless victims of a weakness beyond their control. But that's really not good news for them. And it's not true. You've seen the television ads urging addicts to get help for their problem, to phone that toll-free number. Obviously, addictive behavior is avoidable, not like diseases for which you have no choice about getting help. Alcoholics are not helpless victims in the same way the people they hurt are victimized.

So, thank God, alcoholics can live without the bottle. Let's encourage them that they *can* change. The power of Jesus can help us overcome all of life's challenges. When we unite our will with God's strength, we can do all things through Christ.

Remember the story Christ told about the prodigal son? That young man abandoned his father and left home for a far-off land, where he wasted himself with wild living. Finally, the Bible says, he "came to himself." In other words, he confronted his situation. Then he made the big decision (Luke 15:18): "I will arise and go to my father, and I will say to him, 'Father, I have sinned against heaven and before you'" (RSV).

No more fooling around here. No more excuses. The prodigal took full responsibility for his drunken carousing and called it sin: "I have sinned," he said. Then he did something about it—he took action and went home. You know the story. The father ran to welcome his repentant son, forgiving him fully and freely with the pronouncement (Luke 15:24): "This my son was dead, and is alive again; he was lost, and is found."

Notice that the son had been lost, spiritually dead. Not just sick but dead lost. Thank the Lord, though, now that the boy had confronted his addictive behavior and come home to his father, he was alive and safe.

Let me tell you a story that really touched my heart. It's in that bestselling classic by Dr. James Dobson, *Love Must Be Tough*.

Paul Powers had been a victim of child abuse. Both his mother and father were alcoholics. When he was seven years old, his mother came home drunk from a party and collapsed in the snow before their front door. She caught pneumonia and became deathly sick.

One afternoon she called Paul to her bedside. He got there just in time to watch her die. The boy ran sobbing to his drunken father to tell him what had happened.

"Shut up!" he shouted, pushing the boy away. "Boys don't cry like babies."

The raging man then proceeded to break his son's nose, shatter two of his ribs, and knock out some of his teeth. That was just the beginning of years of escalating abuse for that poor, motherless boy.

At the age of twelve, Paul emerged from his alcoholic environment and committed his first murder. The judge asked Paul's father what he wanted done with the boy. He replied, "Send him to hell!"

Can you imagine! So, young Paul went behind bars with his hate and resentment. Five years later, someone visited the prison with a Billy Graham film, and for the first time, Paul met Jesus. The love of God melted his heart and won him to repentance.

Upon his release from prison, Paul married a fellow believer, and they began a little ministry distributing Christian films. Times were tough financially. When Christmas season came, all they had to their name was eight dollars for groceries.

Paul's wife went to the store with those few precious dollars and came home, having spent one of them on some gold wrapping paper. Paul became furious at what he perceived as her extravagance. While he and his wife argued, their three-year-old daughter sifted through the bag of groceries. Delighted at discovering the wrapping paper, she took it to the living room and proceeded to cover a shoe box.

Well, Paul saw his daughter sitting on the floor cutting up that wrapping paper, and his temper flew off again. Resorting to behavior he himself suffered as a child, he grabbed the little one and hit her violently. Then he sent her sobbing to her room.

The next day, when the family exchanged their few gifts, Paul's daughter ran behind the tree and retrieved her gold box. She handed it to him with a happy smile. "Daddy, this is for you!"

He unwrapped the paper and lifted the lid to find the box completely empty.

"Why did you give me an empty box?" he asked.

"Daddy!" the little one protested. "The box is not empty! It's full of love and kisses for you. I stood there and blew kisses in there for my daddy, and I put love in there too. And it's for you!"

Well, Paul broke down in tears, taking that precious little girl into his arms. For years afterward, he kept her gold box beside his bed. Whenever he felt hurt or discouraged, he reached into the box and lifted out an imaginary kiss from his child. Then he would place it on his cheek and say, "Thank You, Lord."

My friend reading these pages, if you are struggling to overcome an alcoholic environment, the experience of Paul Powers shines hope in your pathway. What the Lord did for him, He can do for you too. He can rebuild your heart and your home, and He wants to begin just now.

Chapter 2

Overcoming a Handicap

February 19, 1981, began as any other day for Terry Wilks. As the Tennessee teenager left for classes, he had no idea it would be his last day of life as he had always lived it. That afternoon an accident at school broke his neck and left him permanently paralyzed.

Eighteen-year-old Terry Wilks loved sports and enjoyed many friends, much like any high-school senior. But Terry stood out from the crowd. Fellow classmates voted him "Most Courteous," along with "Most Likely to Succeed," and also "Best All-Around Gymnast."

A fine Christian upbringing, no doubt, set the stage for success in Terry's life. And the young man made his own personal choice to have Jesus Christ as the center of his life. His fervent faith didn't prevent tragedy from coming his way, however.

On the morning of the accident, Terry's alarm wakened him at the usual time—5:30. He didn't have to get up that early, but he wanted plenty of time for studying his Bible and for prayer. The passage Terry studied that morning had significance for him of which he was unaware—chapter 12 in the Gospel of John, with the anguished words of Jesus shortly before His crucifixion (John 12:27, 28):

"Now is my soul troubled. And what shall I say? 'Father, save me from this hour'? No, for this purpose I have come to this hour. Father, glorify thy name" (RSV).

"Father, glorify thy name." That was the theme of Terry's life too. Having entrusted himself to God for the day, the young man hurriedly dressed and raced to the kitchen. There he wolfed down two bowls of oatmeal.

"Thanks for the breakfast, Mom," he yelled while heading out the door. "See you this afternoon."

His sophomore sister, Diane, was just old enough to start driving. Terry let her take the wheel on their way to Highland Academy, the Seventh-day Adventist secondary school they attended. There they spent the morning working and the afternoon in classes.

Wilks Publications, owned by the parents of Terry and Diane, employed fifteen students on campus. That morning Terry carried stacks of pages from the press to the sorting room. Noontime brought him to the crowded campus cafeteria for lunch with his friends. That afternoon in history class, Terry fought the temptation to fall asleep. Finally, at four o'clock, classes were finished for the day.

"Come on," Terry called to one of his friends. "We're going to be late for practice."

Together they jogged to the gym. After changing clothes, they took their warm-up laps. Then the coach called all the students together for the prayer that always preceded gymnastics practice.

Terry rubbed the chalk brick over his calloused hands and headed for the parallel bars. After twenty-five minutes of swinging and spinning above the mats, Terry decided to do some vaulting. This was the most exciting of all the gymnastic routines for Terry. When he hit the springboard after a fast running start, he felt like a jet taking off.

Terry did a series of front flips off the springboard. Then, flushed with energy, he called to a friend nearby, "Let's try a double!"

Attempting a double front flip was quite risky. Terry wasn't reckless—he just didn't realize the danger involved. He loved to try new things, always pushing himself to higher attainments.

So it was on that fateful afternoon that Terry lined up on the runway. "Arms loose," he reminded himself. "Long strides. Speed is crucial. At the top of the jump, knees to chest. Flip once. Stay tucked. Flip twice. Don't unravel too soon."

With all this in mind, Terry took off. Hitting the springboard at full speed, he soared toward the rafters above. His first flip went well, but then he unraveled too soon and landed on his shoulders.

Not one to give up, Terry shook off the pain and rose to try again. As he lined up for his second attempt, his watch read 5:23. With determination, he raced down the runway and executed his launch. So far, so good; his first flip went as planned. But when he spun into his second flip, his tuck once again loosened too soon. That split-second misjudgment cost him dearly.

Terry had barely started his second flip when his forehead slammed into the mat and snapped backward, while the momentum of his flip carried his body forward. Something in his neck popped. He collapsed in a heap of helplessness.

Hot, searing pain soared through his body. His legs felt cramped, as if someone had put him in a skintight sleeping bag. He couldn't move.

"What's wrong, Terry!" his friends shrieked in horror. "Are you all right?"

"Don't touch him!" the coach warned.

Somebody summoned emergency medical help and called Terry's parents. As his stretcher was carried outside to the chill evening air, classmates crowded around. Despite Terry's overwhelming pain, he tried to smile at them.

"Just remember," he said, "I love you all."

Cars on the lawn formed a circle, headlights lighted to mark a landing zone for the ambulance helicopter. During the flight to Memorial Hospital in Nashville, Terry suffered unbearable pain.

"Please, God, let me black out," he prayed.

The emergency room doctor was compassionate but crisp. He didn't mince words: "Terry's spinal cord is severed or severely damaged. He has no response in his arms and legs." Then came the really awful news: "There's a 90 percent chance he's going to stay this way."

Myrna, Terry's mother, tried to console herself. "Surely he'll be better in the morning."

But, no, Terry wasn't better in the morning. Nor the next day or the next. Gradually the realization sank in that Terry was paralyzed for life. He was a quadriplegic, unable to ever move his limbs again.

Where was God in all this? As Terry's mind writhed in the agony of pain and despair, he thought of Christ's words that he had read the morning of his accident: "Now is my soul troubled. And what shall I say? 'Father, save me from this hour'? No, . . . Father, glorify thy name."

Terry resolved to honor the Lord in the midst of his pain, but nagging questions remained: "Why did God let it happen? Am I being punished somehow? And what about my future—am I doomed to waste the rest of my days in helplessness, hopelessness, and uselessness?"

Such was the turmoil that swirled in Terry's mind as he began the grueling process of recovery, retraining his faculties in various hospitals and centers.

It was a long way back—actually, Terry could never recover normal physical health. As long as he lived, he would have to wrestle with his handicap.

Can you imagine a life like that? Many of you don't have to imagine it—every hour of every day you suffer the pain and hardship of a crippling handicap. No doubt you've wondered many times, Why me? I try to be a good person. Why does God let me suffer like this?

There are many questions for which we will never have answers this side of eternity. In heaven we will see how God has been merciful in ways that we never understood. And speaking of God's mercy for us, actually, none of us are worthy of anything—not even the air we breathe. The Bible does not flatter human nature. It says all of us have sinned and continually fall short of God's glorious ideal. Still He loves us. He gave the supreme sacrifice, Jesus, who became our salvation. And beyond that, He lavishes us with His tender love in our daily living, turning every situation for our good. One of Terry Wilks's favorite verses is Romans 8:28 (NIV): "We know that in all things God works for the good of those who love him, who have been called according to his purpose."

Well, if God is always at work in bringing us good, what about healing? Would God heal Terry?

He certainly has the power; we know that from the way Jesus healed people when He walked this earth. The question is this: Will He always use His healing power the way we want Him to, the way we think He should? Some Christians who promote faith healing say yes, God will definitely heal all illness and infirmities as soon as we have faith.

I do believe in divine healing—the Bible teaches it. And I've seen situations where the genuine healing power of God rescued sick ones from the brink of death. But I've also seen many true believers die, despite their magnificent faith. And you have too, haven't you?

Even the apostle Paul, mighty in faith, found himself perplexed when divine healing failed to come his way. He couldn't persuade the Lord to heal him of a mysterious physical affliction, which he called a "thorn in the flesh." Finally he accepted his handicap, whatever it was, and went on with life. He testified that God allowed his physical condition as a blessing and would indeed bring good out of it.

Keep in mind that Paul's lack of healing didn't mean he lacked faith. You recall he even had faith to raise a man from death (something faith healers today seem unable to do).

Faith in Jesus Christ is the difference between life and death, both here in this world, and for eternity. We can do all things through Christ, who gives us strength.

There are nearly forty million Americans who need the special help of Jesus in dealing with physical disabilities. But, actually, all of us are handicapped in one way or another. We all have our particular weaknesses and vulnerabilities, so we all need the special help of God every day.

Dave Dravecky, a devoted Christian, delighted in entrusting his life to God every morning. If you are a baseball fan, you probably know what happened to the former pitcher for the San Francisco Giants. When a cancerous tumor in his arm threatened to cut short his career, Dave did not selfishly demand to be healed. Instead, he committed himself to God's will, and his quiet faith was a witness to millions.

God worked a miracle for Dave Dravecky. Although his cancer operation required the removal of most of the muscle he used for pitching, against all odds he came back to win again. Thousands of San Francisco fans cheered wildly when he took the mound again at Candlestick Park. Incredibly, he even won the game!

Dave Dravecky was back! What a miracle! But the comeback miracle lasted less than a week. Dave was playing in Montreal, winning the game, when suddenly—as he was pitching—his arm broke. He collapsed in a heap at the foot of the mound. The whole crowd heard that awful snap of the bone.

As they carried Dave off the field, he quietly affirmed his faith in God. And that faith did not waver during long months of uncertainty. Finally, doctors determined that they had no choice but to amputate his arm, and they did.

Did Dave become bitter when God did not heal him, leaving him with a lifelong handicap?

Not at all. Secular sportswriters around the country marveled at his faith, solid as a rock. May I suggest that it took more faith for Dave Dravecky to maintain his trust in the God who apparently failed him than it would have taken for him to demand healing? I believe God displayed a miracle greater than physical healing in the amazing display of Dave's contented commitment.

Millions around the world are acquainted with another life of miracles, Joni Earickson Tada. You may have heard her give her testimony at Billy Graham crusades. We've also been privileged to host her on the "It Is Written" telecast.

A teenage swimming accident left Joni's body paralyzed permanently. For a while, her faith was paralyzed too. She couldn't understand why God allowed such a tragedy. She claimed the gift of divine healing, but nothing seemed to happen. Finally, she resolved that life must go on, and by faith in God she would conquer the challenge of her handicap.

Joni perfected the art of painting with a brush in her mouth. And beyond that, she launched the international ministry, *Joni & Friends*. Her daily radio program ministers to thousands of people, both those who are physically challenged and those normally endowed.

Joni's example meant much to Terry Wilks in his recovery process. She blazed a trail of faith and faithfulness that he determined to follow. The day he met her in person was one of the highlights of his life.

Full of courage, Terry decided to move ahead with college. He attended Southern College near Collegedale, Tennessee, a Seventh-day Adventist institution. A delightful experience awaited him there. He made many friends while prospering in his studies, preparing him for the active life he leads today.

By the way, you can read the complete story of Terry Wilks in his book, *Terry: Follow Your Heart,* available from the publishers of this book.

Through all his trials and tribulations, Terry has been growing spiritually. While he enjoys a fulfilling life here and now despite his handicap, he longs for the time when God will restore to him a healthy body for eternity. One of his favorite Bible passages is the fifteenth chapter of 1 Corinthians. Notice these verses (1 Corinthians 15:51-53):

> Behold, I tell you a mystery: We shall not all sleep, but we shall all be changed—in a moment, in the twinkling of an eye, at the last trumpet. For the trumpet will sound, and the dead will be raised incorruptible, and we shall be changed. For this corruptible must put on incorruptible, and this mortal must put on immortality.

The Bible says death is a sleep that lasts till the resurrection. When the trumpet sounds, millions of tombs will burst open. Then the saints who are watching the dead come to life will find their own bodies instantly transformed into perfection and immortality.

Just think! You'll be standing there, perhaps with arthritis and crutches, and the next moment you'll be leaping for joy in eternal health and youth!

I'm not just imagining this. The Bible guarantees it! (Isaiah 35:5, 6, 10):

> Then the eyes of the blind shall be opened, and the ears of the deaf shall be unstopped. Then the lame shall leap like a deer, . . . and the ransomed of the Lord shall return, and come to Zion with singing, with everlasting joy on their heads. They shall obtain joy and gladness, and sorrow and sighing shall flee away.

I'm looking forward to that—aren't you? God will resurrect His sleeping saints and transform the bodies of those who are alive.

When will this resurrection and transformation happen? Let's go back to 1 Corinthians 15 (verses 22, 23): "As in Adam all die, even so in Christ all shall be made alive. But each one in his own order: Christ the firstfruits, afterward those who are Christ's at His coming."

So it's at the coming of Christ that all God's people will be made alive again. The second coming of our Lord and Saviour Jesus—that's our blessed hope!

Let me tell you about my personal experiences in helping physically challenged people cope and overcome. During my days as a pastor, I conducted Bible classes at a crippled children's home. Whatever God may have helped me contribute there, I think I was the one enriched the most. Some of the most moving experiences of my ministry came through my acquaintance with people like Joanie, Doris, and Jimmy.

Joanie was paralyzed—from her neck down—yet she managed to organize a weekly study, turning pages of the Bible with her tongue! Afterward my children sat on Joanie's lap while she took them for rides in her electric wheelchair.

Doris was paralyzed *and* blind. But she could sing for Jesus, and she did with all her heart.

Jimmy had serious disabilities of his own. He couldn't wait for Jesus to come so he could run and jump and play for all eternity. I think of the day he pleaded, eyes shining with anticipation: "Tell me about heaven!"

"But, Jimmy," I laughed, "we studied about heaven last week."

"I know," he said, "but tell me again!"

That afternoon while driving home, I got to thinking. Suppose I were an atheist who didn't believe in heaven. What hope would I be able to offer Jimmy? And what real encouragement would I have for Joanie? What about blind Doris—if there were no God, no faith, no future eternity—what could I tell her?

Thank God, heaven *is* real! Jesus is real! If we will entrust our lives to Him, we can all live together with our Lord in perfect health and happiness through all eternity. Meanwhile, in this old world, if you find yourself struggling with physical disabilities, take heart. Sooner or later, God will heal you! If not before, then surely when Jesus comes on that resurrection morning.

Will you stretch out your faith and accept whatever plan God has for your life? Will you entrust yourself completely to His care?

Chapter 3

Overcoming Spousal Abuse

The beatings began ten months after the wedding. And for the next fourteen years, Robert Tisland intensified the abuse of his wife and their five children.

Finally, one afternoon, Lucille Tisland couldn't take it anymore. She entered the room where her husband was taking a nap and tiptoed over to the bed. Then she reached under the pillow and slipped out the gun Robert always kept here. With trembling hands she took aim and squeezed the trigger. She shot him dead.

The peaceful Minnesota community where the Tislands lived was shocked. Lucille's many friends had always respected her as a devout Christian. And her husband, whom she killed, was their pastor.

Sunday after Sunday, Robert Tisland pounded the pulpit and mesmerized his congregation. Then, during the week, he menaced his family as a heartless tyrant. At the dinner table, if he didn't like the food his wife cooked, he promptly dumped it on the floor. That didn't hurt anything but Lucille's feelings. The real damage came from Robert's relentless physical abuse. As the years went on, the beatings became increasingly brutal.

One day Robert came home in an especially bad mood. He announced that he was going to take a nap.

33

"When I wake up," he warned Lucille, "I'm going to kill you." The deadly determination in his eyes convinced her he meant business. She decided to save her life by killing him first.

As her tormentor lay dying, Lucille took their sons to a friend's house. Then she returned home, called the police, and waited for them to arrest her. The authorities charged her with murder. Her case went to court, but in March of 1984, a jury acquitted her after hearing her heart-rending story.

Lucille Tisland has plenty of fellow sufferers among abused wives. The FBI estimates that every fifteen seconds someone is abused in America. And they aren't all taking it sitting down anymore—a few, like Lucille, are striking back. Every year 800 to 1,200 women kill the men who abuse them. Most wounded wives just suffer in silence, hoping someday the abuse will stop. But it doesn't.

Should battered wives just commit themselves to God and suffer on? Is that the will of God for them? Or does He want them to take action to escape their abusive spouse? Let's look for guiding principles in the Bible.

First, we must understand exactly what spousal abuse is. It happens when the mate, usually the wife, becomes the victim of physical assault, threats of violence, or emotional abuse—including ridicule and demeaning behavior. You would think that living in a religious environment would provide shelter from abuse. But not necessarily. Believe it or not, some psychologists suggest that up to 80 percent of abuse takes place in religious homes.

Here's another disturbing statistic. Domestic abuse is so common that about half the couples in the United States experience violence at some time in their marriage. In times of unusual stress, perhaps, people may find themselves arguing a lot. Some men, finding themselves on the short end of verbal logic, lash out physically and hit their wives.

No matter how much pressure a man may be under, there's no excuse for this abuse. Violence in the home cannot be tolerated. Some abusive husbands recognize this and feel deep remorse, determining to never hit their wives again. And sometimes they don't—but all too often the abuse becomes a common occurrence.

The typical abuser does not go around town like a monster or a borderline criminal. He may be your favorite physician or that charming college professor—perhaps even your beloved pastor, like Robert Tisland. We'll get back to the tragic experience of the Tislands later.

Let's ask a basic question about spousal abuse. Why do men who appear to be respectable, responsible husbands become abusers—why do they go on year after year secretly battering their wives?

For one thing, beneath all their macho-style bluster, abusers are basically insecure people who consider anyone who crosses their path to be a personal threat. Like the man I'll call Ed, who battered his wife Mary. Ed resisted any of Mary's suggestions or ideas, dismissing them as a threat to his leadership. "Quit nagging me!" he would yell. He also raged over any supposed neglect on her part, even an obviously innocent oversight. With this rough attitude, you see, he was trying to compensate for his own feelings of inadequacy.

As you might expect, Ed's insecurity made him intensely jealous of Mary. Early in their relationship, his need for her constant attention made her feel desirable. As time went on, though, she grew wary of his demands for exclusive attention and his constant suspicion. Ed often accused Mary of having affairs, and this imagined infidelity provided him an excuse to beat her up.

Abusers, partly out of their insecurity, share a common need to control their environment. Robert Tisland, for instance, was a classic manipulator. At first his confident, take-charge attitude made Lucille feel secure. Here was a man who would never fail to guide her and provide for her, she thought. After a while, however, Robert's control of her life became suffocating. He wouldn't let Lucille leave the house without getting permission from him. He made her beg for money and monitored everything she spent. Not that she had much money to keep track of—mostly a few dimes and quarters he allowed her for phone calls. After a while, Robert even demanded that Lucille call him "Sir" or "Pastor." Can you imagine! One of Robert's favorite admonitions to her was, "It's not yours to question why. It's yours to do or die."

Obey me or die? What was the source of such incredible arrogance? Like many religious men—hypocrites, I'm afraid—Robert Tisland misapplied certain Bible passages that instruct wives to be submissive to their husbands. Such men actually believe that the Lord intends their wives to be their slaves.

Is this the will of God for the marriage relationship? Let's find out what the Bible really says (Ephesians 5:22-24):

> Wives, submit to your own husbands, as to the Lord. For the husband is head of the wife, as also Christ is head of the church; and He is the Savior of the body. Therefore, just as the church is subject to Christ, so let the wives be subject to their own husbands in everything.

That's where many husbands stop reading. They conveniently overlook the next verse (Ephesians 5:25):

"Husbands, love your wives, just as Christ also loved the church and gave Himself for it."

Yes, the Bible does establish the husband as the leader of the home. But that doesn't make the wife a doormat! Not at all. Husbands are to love their wives—love them in the same way that Jesus loves His church. Jesus gave His life for us—and that's the kind of love the Bible says husbands ought to have for their wives.

Of course, it isn't every day that a husband would lay down his life, literally die, to protect his wife. But every day he must lay down his selfishness and arrogance. His stubbornness and anger must die.

How can that be possible? What can transform an abuser into a loving and lovable spouse?

Well, it isn't easy. It takes nothing short of a miracle. First, the abuser must acknowledge himself as a sinner. Abuse is not masculine leadership—it's a horrible betrayal of the husband's God-given role. It's also a deadly sin of which he must repent or be forever lost.

This experience of repentance involves more than just becoming religious. Robert Tisland, the abusing pastor, was certainly religious. All kinds of international terrorism is conducted under the umbrella of holy war. This world doesn't need more religion—we need the Lord Jesus Christ! And we need Him personally!

The love of Jesus shown at Calvary can humble the hardest heart. But we must contemplate the cross. We must individually allow the love of our Saviour to melt our hardened hearts.

Well, once this love of God has humbled the abuser, and he acknowledges this sin, then what? The next step should be Christian counseling from a qualified professional. The ex-abuser must understand his past behavior so he can prevent its recurrence.

You see, abuse is actually a cycle of three stages: First, there is the tension-building stage, so familiar to every battered spouse. Some incident triggers the wrath of the abuser. He gets that certain look in his eye, and even without words being spoken, you can tell trouble is coming. Then it happens—violence erupts—that's the second stage. Finally, the storm is over, and then comes the third stage, remorse. The raging lion might suddenly become a whimpering lamb. The abuser bubbles over with apologies. Sometimes he overwhelms his victim with gifts. He may get down on his knees and promise never to hit her again.

Past experience should demonstrate the worthlessness of all those promises to reform. Things don't get better. Battering is a pattern that usually gets worse and worse without some kind of crisis intervention or escape. So the victim must not allow her tormentor to manipulate her emotions by empty expressions of sorrow, mingled with what amounts to crocodile tears. She must insist that her husband prove his repentance by submitting to professional counseling.

A good counselor will require the abuser to accept responsibility and deal with the root problems we talked about—insecurity and low self-worth. The abusive husband must learn to resolve his stress without resorting to violence. He needs to develop communication skills so he can express himself with his words rather than with his fists. The ultimate solution for the abuser is to be born again, to surrender to God's forgiving, healing love.

Now let's turn our attention to the victim of abuse. What made her get involved with such a dangerous man in the first place? And why does she stay with him through year after year of abuse, doing nothing about it?

Well, many wives face danger or even death if they try to escape. It was that way for Lucille Tisland before she killed her husband. She recalls, "I was scared of leaving Robert because he had threatened that if I ever left he would come and find me and the boys, and all that would be left would be pieces."

Can you imagine what it must have been like to live under such circumstances? Tragically, some of you already do. If so, please read this carefully. You are not helpless. Abuse against your body is a crime in our society. It's true that police have been traditionally reluctant to get involved in domestic assaults, but more and more, that's changing. And that's good news. Here's some more—statistics show that when abusive spouses are reported to the police, they are less likely to maintain their violence than if their crime goes unreported. So despite her husband's threats, a battered wife is safer if she reports him to the police than if she doesn't.

But suppose the abuse does get worse after she calls the police? Then to protect her life and any children involved, she needs to escape the situation.

Back in the time of the ancient Hebrews, the Lord directed that certain places should be set apart as sanctuaries where people in danger could flee. We read about them in Numbers 35:12: "They shall be cities of refuge for you from the avenger."

These ancient cities of refuge were especially designed as a place of escape for suspected murderers so they could survive the wrath of the victim's family long enough to receive a fair trial. Now tell me—if a suspected murderer deserved a place of refuge, how much more a helpless family being abused?

Thank God, many communities and churches have made provision for sheltering battered families. Along with food and a place to sleep in peace, these shelters provide counseling services, child care, financial and legal assistance—often medical help as well. If you want information about these shelters of refuge, you can call the toll-free National Domestic Hotline for a local shelter referral: 1-800-873-7233.

Many battered wives are reluctant to escape for fear they would have no permanent place to live after they leave the temporary shelter. To prevent this, laws have been passed to protect property rights and guarantee the income of abused spouses. These days, abused families are often awarded their home, and the abuser is forced to get out. Such an arrangement ought to be ordered by the court before the victims leave their temporary shelter. Naturally, abusers don't appreciate having to move out and find themselves someplace else to live, but any violation of such a court order makes them subject to arrest. That's usually enough to make them leave their battered family alone.

Here's an important caution for wives who have been abused—don't be overly anxious to welcome the abuser back home before he has truly changed. He may bombard you with all kinds of promises. He may manipulate you with guilt, accusing you of being unforgiving if you don't immediately take him back. Demand that he first complete a series of counseling sessions—often these can be arranged by the court. Then, if the counselor determines that he has sincerely changed his ways, you can risk taking him back. But don't burn your bridges—tell the repentant spouse that things must never become violent again.

Speaking of counseling sessions—the battered wife also needs professional help for herself. One woman, Barbara, lamented, "I needed someone to talk to—I didn't know what to do! I blamed myself for what was going on. For so many years I felt afraid, angry, ashamed, guilty, embarrassed, confused, and worthless."

Finally, with the help of God through qualified Christian counseling, Barbara learned to deal with her inner turmoil. Her counselor also helped her recognize the abuse stages so she could attempt to avert the violence. She learned to avoid arguments, especially about sensitive topics, when her husband showed signs of stress. Her counselor also taught her never to ridicule her husband, never question his manhood or compare him with other men. That would only set the stage for trouble.

As I mentioned before, there's never any excuse for violence under any circumstances. But wives can often avoid abusive situations if they know what to do. A qualified counselor can help so much.

There are other reasons why many wives put up with terrible abuse, besides fear of danger or deprivation. Susan, for example, imagined herself as something of a savior to her abusive husband. She convinced herself that through patience and tenderness, she could eventually reform him. That didn't work. Her husband interpreted her meekness as weakness, and that only intensified his appetite for violence.

In other cases, well-meaning friends admonish the battered spouse to remain with her husband for the sake of holding the family together. Often they misapply scriptures that call for us to endure suffering and carry the cross. But God never intended for women and children to suffer emotional and physical devastation. If there is a pattern of abuse in your home, separation of the marriage may be the only answer— at least temporarily, perhaps permanently. And often this is the only way to teach the abuser lessons he will never forget. The terms of a legal separation can guarantee the financial security of the family.

Certainly, the separation of a marriage should not be taken lightly. But in cases where a spouse is abusive, it may be the only sensible option. I've noticed, though, that some wives seem almost addicted to their abusive husbands, as if they couldn't exist without them. At first, such blind loyalty may seem a virtue, but when we think it through, a question confronts us. Does God ever intend that an adult in good health and sound mind should be totally dependent upon someone else?

Keep that question in mind as we read this invitation from Jesus (Matthew 11:28-30).

> Come to Me, all you who labor and are heavy laden, and I will give you rest. Take My yoke upon you and learn from Me, for I am gentle and lowly in heart, and you will find rest for your souls. For My yoke is easy and My burden is light.

What a comforting invitation from our Lord Jesus Christ! "Come to Me," He says. Whatever your suffering may be, Jesus understands your situation. He feels all your pain. And our Lord offers you more than helpless sympathy. "All power in heaven and earth is Mine," Jesus declared—and He isn't abusive with all that infinite power. He is meek and tender, reaching out to help you.

Chapter 4

Overcoming Depression

I wish you could meet Cindy, who once suffered from depression. This is her story:

"It all began when I was a girl and my mother died. I thought she abandoned me because she didn't like me. The next few years, my father moved us around quite a bit. I guess I never had any real friends. I grew up thinking nobody liked me—really cared about me.

"By the time I got to high school, I was depressed most of the time, except when some guy liked me. But sooner or later, we broke up, and I got even more depressed.

"I started thinking about ending my life. I desperately wanted someone to try to stop me. I wanted to know that somebody really cared. It seemed like no one did.

"So, late one night, I got a razor blade and slit my wrists. As soon as I saw blood, I got scared and stopped. I decided I wanted to live after all. The problem is, I'm so depressed, I feel I have nothing to live for."

Poor Cindy. Her experience represents millions of hurting women, men, and children in our world today. And, yes, many of them are sincere, wholehearted Christians. Depression plays no favorites.

More than we realize, people who are part of our everyday lives suffer from depression. Everything may seem fine on the surface. But deep within, there's an overwhelming sadness, hopelessness, and desperation—a severe discouragement that never goes away. Depressed people don't have the energy to do what they want or what they think they ought to be doing. So they feel guilty, especially when they let their loved ones down. They condemn themselves as useless and worthless. And in their lowest moments, they feel like ending it all.

Maybe that's how you've been feeling. If so, my friend, take heart. I have wonderful news for you—there is hope and help available. I can't guarantee any quick solution for depression; many complex factors probably put you where you are. But once you understand the problem, there is a way out—with God's help. You may also need counseling from a qualified Christian professional. But at least with these ideas you can get started on the road to relief.

First of all, keep in mind that you are not suffering alone. Depression haunts thirty to forty million people in the United States alone, not to mention millions more in Europe, Canada, and around the world. It afflicts people of all ages and backgrounds.

Let's probe the causes of depression. Often it can be linked to easily corrected physical problems. I think of John, an architect, who lost a lot of sleep working on a special project. During that time, he failed to eat properly—munching a candy bar and gulping coffee at his desk rather than taking time for lunch. Upon arriving home, he just collapsed in front of the television rather than going for his usual walk. After a few weeks of this, John found himself terribly depressed, even though his work project was moving along on schedule.

You see, lack of sleep can eventually plunge you into depression, especially when combined with other psychological factors I'll mention in a moment. Improper diet—too much sugar along with caffeine, for example, can also contribute to depression. Lack of exercise too. It's amazing how many people escape the doldrums of depression after they get out of the house and take up some sport like tennis—or even half an hour of brisk walking every day.

Other physical factors contributing to depression are illness and the side effects of prescribed medication. Beyond these varied physical aspects are the psychological ones. Like loneliness, for example. You who are single and living alone are well acquainted with temptation to feel sorry for yourself. And the next thing you know, you're depressed.

Of course, you don't have to live alone to be lonely. Some of the loneliest people in the world are young mothers like Cindy, whom we talked about at the beginning of this chapter.

After marrying Tom and having their dream of a baby fulfilled, Cindy thought she'd never again be depressed. But faced with the endless demands of motherhood, she began to feel like a prisoner serving a sentence of solitary confinement within the walls of her apartment.

"If I could only get out into the real world," she imagined, "I'd finally be rid of my loneliness."

Naturally, Cindy always loved her baby, yet she craved something more than just baby talk. Not a single in-depth relationship relieved the monotony of her existence. Daytime game shows and soap operas offered familiar faces but only counterfeit companionship.

Tom, Cindy's husband, could flee the house every morning and head off to work. Cindy imagined him joking with his buddies at the service station while she was lonely at home. She felt sorry for herself, resentful of her husband's freedom to come and go. Before long, Cindy became deeply depressed.

Besides loneliness mingled with self-pity and resentment, another factor contributing to Cindy's depression was stress. Not so much the daily routine of caring for her baby; what got to her were the frequent situations in which she felt out of control. There was the time when her little one kept getting sick. Doctors couldn't figure out the cause of that constant low-grade fever. Cindy felt helpless. She wondered if somehow she had caused her baby's illness. Maybe she wasn't as good a mother as she was supposed to be.

That left her feeling guilty. Guilt, all by itself, can bring on depression. When you feel you have failed or done something wrong, guilt sparks self-condemnation, frustration, hopelessness—and finally depression.

Anger can also get you depressed—anger held within and turned against oneself. Usually, anger is rooted in hurt feelings or disappointment.

Cindy felt hurt when Tom didn't come home from work to help her care for their sick baby. She was disappointed that he stayed out drinking with his friends. After a few such weeks, she became angry at Tom. The only way she knew to let off steam was to yell at him, but that only aggravated him and also upset the baby. So Cindy learned to keep quiet and repress the anger seething within. She wouldn't even admit to herself the fury she felt, so it raged beneath the surface of her consciousness. Such unresolved anger could be the most common cause of depression.

Cindy's experience illustrates the difference between most women and men in the way they deal with anger. Men are more likely to carry out their angry impulses—that's one reason most violent criminals are male. Women don't usually have the opportunity to lash out as men sometimes have. We don't expect them to fight with their fists, and if they attack verbally, they risk inciting physical abuse from their husbands or alienating their in-laws. So many women learn to suffer silently, internalizing their anger. That's how they become victims of depression.

There's one last cause of depression I'll mention—suffering a painful loss such as bankruptcy, divorce, or the death of a loved one. Cindy had never gotten over her mother's death. She found herself angry somehow that her mother went away when she needed her most. Of course, it wasn't her mother's fault that a drunken driver killed her. Cindy knew that, and she blamed herself for having rage that was irrational. You can see how guilt, combined with all the other problems in Cindy's life, plunged her into depression.

Well, now we have a picture of what depression is and how it's caused. That leaves us with the question: How can a sincere child of God suffer bouts with depression?

Throughout the Scriptures we find godly people suffering depression. David, who lived three thousand years ago, was an honored war veteran, talented musician, and the handsome hero of the nation's women. You would think such an illustrious character would be immune to depression. But no—all the factors we discussed that contribute to depression were active in David's life. The book of Psalms, a collection of musical poetry, provides insight into his inner turmoil—loneliness, stress, guilt, anger, and painful loss.

You know about David with his slingshot conquering the enemy giant Goliath. He became a folk hero after that, which made King Saul envious. The angry monarch even tried to murder his young rival. David had to escape through the back window of his home and flee into the desert, pursued by the army. Then the king snatched David's beautiful wife and gave her to another man.

Understandably, the heartbroken newlywed became depressed. He refused to abandon his faith, though, continuing to commit himself into God's care. Here is his heart cry during the depths of his despair (Psalm 43:5): "Why are you cast down, O my soul? And why are you disquieted within me? Hope in God; for I shall yet praise Him, the help of my countenance and my God."

Praise the Lord—whatever our desperate situation, we, too, can find refuge in His mercy. In our darkest hour we can stretch our faith and even sing about His power to save us!

Anyone struggling with depression would benefit from reading the prayers of David. Millions of Christians and Jewish people begin each morning in prayer with the Psalms, finding in them encouragement and strength.

We all like to be encouraged, but I also need to share a warning here. Sometimes depression results from our willful violation of God's law. We cannot escape such guilt by merely praising the Lord—our sin must be confessed and forsaken in order to be forgiven. David's darkest hour came after he stole another man's wife and then tried to cover up the crime with murder. Not until he repented of that sin was he able to rise above the depression that resulted.

Thank the Lord, He is very merciful and eager to pardon any transgression, no matter how serious. His unlimited mercy encouraged David to be totally open about his feelings. I'm particularly intrigued by the way he was honest about his anger. You recall that repressed anger is one of the major causes of depression. Well, rather than keeping his anger within or lashing out and attacking his enemies, David learned to vocalize his anger during prayer.

Often in the Psalms we find him absolutely furious. I used to wonder why some of what he said was even in the Bible! Now I realize God wants to show us He can relate to struggling sinners no matter what our mood may be. However we feel, He loves us just the same and invites us to communicate with Him.

That's quite encouraging, don't you think? Now listen to this (Romans 15:13): "Now may the God of hope fill you with all joy and peace in believing, that you may abound in hope by the power of the Holy Spirit."

So the power of the Holy Spirit comes to us through the hope we have in Christ. Believing in His love provides powerful ammunition against the turbulent emotions that threaten to keep us in the valley of depression.

Loneliness? The Bible assures us that we're never alone—our Lord is always with us, even unto the end of the world. Distressed? In every situation God has promised to work for the good of those who love Him. And whatever losses we may suffer, He will supply our every need according to His riches in Christ Jesus. Guilt? Whatever our failures, there is no condemnation for those who live by faith in Christ Jesus. Anger and resentment? Since God forgives us, we are equipped to forgive those who hurt us and love one another as He loves us.

You can see how the gospel of God's grace provides a powerful antidote to depression. Secular psychology just can't compete with what God can do for us. Unfortunately, human nature is quick to forget what we have in Jesus. That's why the Lord offers us a weekly reminder of the gospel, a powerful weapon against depression—seventh-day Sabbath rest in Christ.

You know how depressing it is to be reminded of our shortcomings. Well, every week God offers us a vacation from all we have failed to accomplish. When the sun goes down Friday evening, He invites us to set aside business as usual of a day to celebrate the wonderful things He offers us in Jesus.

To get the background on Sabbath rest, let's go back to Creation week. As Adam and Eve gaze in awe at the wonders of paradise, the Lord turns it over to their care. But before they take charge of their beautiful Eden home, the Creator sets up a weekly appointment with them. And so we read (Genesis 2:3): "God blessed the seventh day and sanctified it, because in it He rested from all His work which God had created and made."

So God "sanctified," or set apart, the seventh-day Sabbath for His human family to share the celebration of His work. Even though we did nothing to earn the right to rest, God wants us to accept His accomplishment on our behalf.

This Sabbath rest in God's finished work symbolizes what Christianity stands for. Other world religions glorify self-realization, human accomplishment. But Christians celebrate God's accomplishments on our behalf. That's why the Sabbath points us away from ourselves, away from all our unfinished business. It helps us appreciate what God has done.

Our Lord also knew we need a weekly reservation to be with our loved ones, uninterrupted by daily duties. Often family members brush past each other throughout the busy week, out of time and out of touch, nearly strangers in the same home. Each week, the Sabbath offers time off from the cares of life to refresh family relationships.

Are you beginning to see how accepting Sabbath rest can help you overcome depression? Every week you can trade your loneliness for fellowship and worship with your family and friends. As for that helpless feeling of life being out of control, the Sabbath reminds us that we have a God who created this world and still holds it in His mighty hands. This weekly escape from the rat race also soothes the frustration that sparks anger and resentment. Not only that, Sabbath rest relieves guilt by assuring us that despite our failures and shortcomings, we stand complete in Christ, perfect in God's sight. And when we suffer loss, the Sabbath points us forward to the time the Creator will make all things new and restore to us everything we've lost here on earth. Besides all this, of course, the Sabbath provides a great opportunity to refresh ourselves physically by getting out in nature.

What a wonderful boost for body, mind, and soul we find each week in the Sabbath! No wonder the New Testament tells us (Hebrews 4:9, NASB): "There remains therefore a Sabbath rest for the people of God."

Maybe all this is new to you. Why not study it out for yourself? You might want to read our book, *When God Made Rest*, available from the publishers of this book.

Come with me now to the nation of Israel. From the Mediterranean port city of Haifa, we drive eastward through the Valley of Megiddo, following the mountain ridge. Soon we arrive at Mount Carmel. Turning south, we take the winding road up its towering heights.

One day long ago, this mountain hosted a dramatic showdown between God and His enemies. In a time of national emergency, the prophet Elijah summoned the nation here to make their decision between true and false worship. God won a great victory through the fearless leadership of Elijah.

The next day, however, the prophet had an awful letdown after his mountaintop experience. Facing some unexpected opposition, he became afraid and ran for his life. Scripture takes up the account of what happened next (1 Kings 19:4): "He himself went a day's journey into the wilderness, and came and sat down under a broom tree. And he prayed that he might die, and said, 'It is enough! Now, Lord, take my life, for I am no better than my fathers.'"

The ultimate depression—Elijah wished he could die. Having given up on life, the prophet sank into an exhausted sleep. Well, Elijah may have given up on himself, but the Lord hadn't given up on him. He sent an angel to bring him some food.

Still depressed as ever, Elijah took off deeper into the wilderness until he found a cave. He crept inside and crouched in its dark shadows.

There he had an unexpected visitor. God came down to see him—not to scold him for his lack of faith. No, in a quiet, comforting voice, the Lord inquired, "What are you doing here, Elijah? Come out of that dark cave and into the sunlight—I've got special plans for your life."

I don't know what pain and despair you may be feeling today, but Jesus does. He loves you just as much as He loves anyone else. And He knows from personal experience what it's like to suffer pangs of depression. You see, when He was down here on earth, He became lonely too. His closest friends rejected Him. Then His enemies hung Him upon the cross.

All this suffering and rejection Jesus took upon Himself at Calvary so that now—this very day—He can accept you into a thrilling, fulfilling relationship with Him. He will warm your heart with His love and give meaning to your life.

Jesus is calling you—He's calling you out of the darkness of your cave into the sunlight of His love.

Chapter 5

Overcoming Sexual Abuse

It isn't easy for me to tell you what happened to Linda. We don't like to talk about the problem of sexual abuse. We would rather pretend it isn't happening everywhere around us—even in Christian families.

Linda's problem was with her father. How could she ever overcome five years of pain and shame?

When Linda was a little girl, her father seldom found time to spend with her. "Too busy," he said. Too busy watching the ballgame to take her to the park. Too busy with the evening paper to help her with homework. Too busy for just about anything that had to do with Linda—he didn't even attend her school plays. No meaningful personal attention whatsoever.

Suddenly that changed when Linda turned thirteen. Her father began noticing her, paying her compliments. Not one to show affection before, he began hugging her a lot. And when they embraced, his hands began touching her in places they shouldn't have.

Linda felt uncomfortable when this happened—just like you and I feel uncomfortable talking about the tragedy of sexual abuse. But thousands of you reading this are victims of sexual abuse—and many of you have never come to terms with what you've suffered. You try to forget the nightmare, but it's like a faded picture in your wallet carried with you all the time. Your haunted memories poison all your relationships with men, especially your marriage. Can you ever find relief from the pain of the past?

A recent issue of *Los Angeles Times Magazine* featured the cover article "Daddy's Girls," describing a family's tragic encounter with incest. One of the victimized daughters, now an adult, testified before her father: "I didn't trust anyone until . . . the age of forty-one." She continued, "It would have been better to have never known life than to go through what you forced me to go through. The shame and devastation made me want to die."

Her sister added, "If I had my life to live over, I'd say, 'No, I'll pass.'"

I can only try to imagine the pain endured by these women. And the sexual abuse they suffered is a widespread problem in our society. No wonder it's discussed again and again on popular TV talk shows. For a real solution, we need more than the secular, humanistic solutions promoted by pop psychologists. I want to bring you a sound, Christ-centered solution based upon God's Word.

First, we must understand more about the problem of sexual abuse. It's far more rampant than we might imagine. A recent survey indicated that 38 percent of women interviewed had been sexually abused by the age of eighteen. Can you believe it—nearly four out of ten! And most shocking of all, many who have suffered sexual mistreatment don't even realize they have been victims. Most of them quietly blame themselves for what happened.

Please understand this. It's not just forced physical sexual contact that constitutes abuse. A girl might be violated by the apparently affectionate fondling of a favorite uncle who can't keep his hands off her body.

You see, sexual abuse isn't necessarily a painful or frightening experience. Actually, it doesn't always involve physical contact; it can be verbal or even visual harassment, such as teasing about sexual things, perhaps an obscene comment, or a leering, lingering stare.

So any type of inappropriate sexual attention is sexual abuse. And from an adult toward a minor, any sexual communication whatever—whether resisted or not—is a crime.

Now, I've been focusing on the sexual abuse of females. Millions of males are victims too. But the most serious problem we have is the abuse of women, such as the experience with Linda we've been discussing. You understand, of course, that I've changed her name and circumstances to protect her privacy.

As I mentioned, Linda felt uncomfortable about her father fondling her. Even so, after years of neglect, it felt so good to finally have his arms around her—so she tried not to think about what his hands were doing.

Then one morning during summer vacation, the abuse escalated. Linda's mother had left the house to go shopping, and Linda was in her bedroom getting dressed. Without warning, the door opened, and in walked her father. Then he made her have sex with him.

Linda protested, but her father would not be denied. He wasn't rough with her, just insistent that she submit to his sexual advances.

So began five years of horrible incest. The abuse was relentless, yet gentle, even tender. Linda's father pampered her, treating her like his lover. He confided that their secret relationship meant more to him than his marriage. In fact, he said the only thing keeping him home with her mother was this so-called "love" they "shared."

At first, Linda was repulsed at the thought of taking her mother's place in her father's arms. But as time went on, he convinced her that she was a family hero by keeping the home from breaking up. She began to think of herself as quite grown up, wise beyond her years. After a couple of years she even got a bit smug, almost relishing her role as Mother's secret rival.

All this changed when Linda was a high-school senior. When her sex-education class discussed the crime of incest, she became disillusioned about the perverted relationship she had with her father. She tried to persuade him to stop.

He wouldn't. He said she belonged to him, and he intended to keep her. When Linda persisted in her protests, her father threatened to ruin her life if she exposed what he called their "little secret." Linda knew she could have him arrested, but she was afraid she would turn everybody's life upside down. She thought of confiding in her mother or her teacher but decided against it. Instead, immediately after high-school graduation, Linda fled from her dungeon of incest. It was too late—her emotions were in ruins.

Linda had a shotgun wedding with a fellow she hardly knew, and of course the marriage didn't last. Divorce came within a year or two. Hoping to rebuild her life, Linda moved to the state capital. She landed a well-paying job as a receptionist, which afforded her glamorous clothes and a shiny sports car.

Well, Linda had an exciting new lifestyle, but it failed to bring new life to her shattered soul. She could get no satisfaction from material things or superficial relationships. Searching for more, she eventually found herself drawn to spiritual things. She started watching Christian television programs. One weekend she wandered into church, where she enrolled in a weekly Bible study.

As Linda learned about God's Word, she felt dirty inside and guilty about what had happened at home. And something else troubled her. At one point a few years back, she had become pregnant by her father. He quickly arranged an abortion, and, despite misgivings, Linda cooperated. Now it all came back to haunt her.

With so much guilt stirring up the mud in her conscience, Linda felt terrible about herself. She regretted going to church. She had hoped she might find comfort from God there, but now she felt under His curse. Linda got depressed, almost suicidal.

She knew she had to do something or talk to someone. Mustering her courage, she called the pastor for an appointment. There in his office, she sobbed out the whole ugly story.

Linda expected the man of God to scold her or at least preach a sermon. Instead, he listened empathetically, assuring her that her Father in heaven loved her, and so did her new church family.

Having said that, the pastor looked thoughtfully out the window for a while. Then he turned to face Linda again. "The first thing I have to ask you is whether you have any sisters at home your father might be abusing."

"No," Linda replied. "I'm the youngest, and my other sisters are already married."

"You understand that your father committed a crime against you. You really should have reported him. Not for the sake of revenge, but to protect yourself as well as to help him—he needs counseling."

"You're right, pastor, I should have put a stop to the relationship. I'm to blame for letting it go on like it did."

"Now, wait a minute, Linda. That affair was fundamentally your father's fault. He got it started, he kept it going, he refused to break it off."

"But I have to admit that what my father did to me—well, it felt good. You know, all that fondling and caressing."

"Linda," explained the pastor, "the way our bodies are created, if certain parts are stimulated, of course it feels good. That's a simple biological reality."

"What you're saying makes sense, pastor," Linda replied. "But I still feel guilty about letting my father abuse me without reporting him. And besides—after a while, I stopped resisting him. I found myself cooperating, even looking forward to our encounters together. I actually enjoyed what we were doing. I'm afraid I'm not an innocent victim."

"Linda, I'm not suggesting you are totally innocent. All of us are sinners, the Bible says, guilty before God. So you may indeed share some responsibility for what went on over the years before you managed to break it off. Well, then, confess yourself to God as a sinner, and then move on with life.

"Listen to this," the pastor said, reaching for his Bible.

" 'All we like sheep have gone astray; we have turned, every one, to his own way; and the Lord has laid on Him the iniquity of us all' (Isaiah 53:6).

"Jesus paid it all, Linda. On the cross He paid the full price of our sin. Now we can stand clean before God."

"That's almost too good to believe," Linda said, wiping a tear away. "I can hardly believe God would forgive me so completely. But I don't know if I could ever forgive myself."

"Linda," the pastor admonished, "who gave you the right to forgive yourself or to condemn yourself? That's something only God can do as the Judge of all the earth. Are you putting yourself in the place of God?"

The young woman looked stunned for a moment. "I never thought of it that way."

"Notice this here," the pastor said, turning to Romans 8:33, 34: "'Who shall bring a charge against God's elect? It is God who justifies. Who is he who condemns? It is Christ who dies, and furthermore is also risen, who is even at the right hand of God, who also makes intercession for us.'

"God the Judge justifies you, forgives you," the pastor said. "Nobody can condemn you. You don't even have the right to condemn yourself!"

"You're right!" Linda responded. She actually started laughing. "That's terrific, pastor. I love it!"

Then a perplexed look clouded her face. "The verse you just read said Jesus 'intercedes' for us. Why does He need to do that for us if God isn't out to condemn us?"

A good question, wouldn't you say? Something vital to understand. And the Bible leaves no doubt about it. It's the devil who's the accuser of the brethren. The enemy of our souls tries to incriminate us before God day and night. I'm sure he's jealous about our going to heaven, where he used to live when he was Lucifer, prince of the angels. And so he accuses us of being unqualified to pass through the pearly gates.

"But," you exclaim, "we are unworthy, aren't we? How do we counter those accusations of the enemy?"

Notice what the Bible says (Revelation 12:11): "They overcame him by the blood of the Lamb."

Oh, friend, do you see it? It's through the blood of Jesus that you and I overcome the devil's accusations. In the judgment, God takes our side against the enemy. He has appointed Jesus to assist Him, interceding in our defense against the accusations of Satan.

Let's probe this a little deeper. To really understand the judgment, we must get back to the ancient legal system of Old Testament times. Back then, the Hebrew court system differed drastically from ours. To begin with, we read in the *Jewish Encyclopedia*,

"Attorneys at law are unknown in Jewish law."[1]
Witnesses of the crime pressed charges. And who
defended the accused? The judge! Hebrew law required judges to "lean always to the side of the
defendant and give him the advantage of every possible doubt."[2]

Only when overwhelmed by evidence could the judge
abandon his defense of the accused and reluctantly pronounce condemnation. The judge, obviously, was more
than a neutral guardian of justice. He took the side of
the accused and was biased in favor of acquittal.

So God, as our Judge, takes our defense! But doesn't
He also have to be fair—even though He wants to
forgive us?

Well, certainly He can't deny Satan's contention
that we are sinful. But in the blood shed on Calvary's
cross, He has the evidence He needs to pronounce us
innocent. So He dismisses Satan's charges, endorsing
the security in Christ we have enjoyed since we
accepted Him.

God is on our side! I'm glad for that, and I know you
are too. He's not only *on* our side during the judgment;
He's also *at* our side down here, giving us strength, day
by day, to obey His will and keep His commandments.
He will bring harmony to our confusion and give us
new life in Jesus.

All this the pastor explained to Linda that day in his
office.

"That sounds just wonderful," she told him. "If only
I could start life all over, living it God's way. I wish I
were a virgin again."

The pastor replied, "I have good news for you. When
you accept Jesus, you *are* a virgin in God's sight. Listen
to this: 'If anyone is in Christ, he is a new creation; old
things have passed away; behold, all things have
become new' (2 Corinthians 5:17).

"Do you want that new beginning Jesus has for you? Well, praise God, the good news is even better than you think. You see, new life in Jesus means more than just a new start. The Bible says: 'You are complete in Him' (Colossians 2:10).

"When you accept Jesus, God doesn't see you as a struggling spiritual baby. He sees you as already perfect. He looks down from heaven at you, and He smiles, saying, 'This is Charles, my beloved son, in whom I am well pleased. This is Linda, my beloved daughter, in whom I am well pleased.'

"I want to take full advantage of such a wonderful opportunity in Christ, and I know you do too. To begin with, confess your sins to the Lord—acknowledge yourself as a sinner. Then, in Jesus' name, just banish any trace of guilt. In case you still don't *feel* forgiven, don't worry about it. You *know* you are forgiven because God promises to accept us when we come to Him in Christ."

Well, together the pastor and Linda bowed in prayer and she accepted Jesus as her Saviour and Lord. It was the beginning of a whole new life for her. No, it wasn't easy. In the weeks and months ahead, she had many struggles. The pastor recommended a licensed Christian counselor, who proved to be quite helpful in her recovery.

That's Linda's story. Now, what about you—have you been the victim of sexual abuse? You need the healing love of Jesus. Listen to this thrilling promise from God's Word:

> Seeing then that we have a great High Priest who has passed through the heavens, Jesus the Son of God, let us hold fast our confession. For we do not have a High Priest who cannot sympathize with our weaknesses, but was in

all points tempted as we are, yet without sin. Let us therefore come boldly to the throne of grace, that we may obtain mercy and find grace to help in time of need (Hebrews 4:14-16).

Think of it! In Jesus, God offers us mercy to forgive our sins and shortcomings. And more—in Christ, we have grace to help us in time of need. Whenever tempted, we need not fall prey to the devil's devices. God has strength to keep us from lapsing into the old patterns of abuse and defeat.

Did you notice something interesting in that text we just read, something personal for you? It says Jesus is your great High Priest. This opens the door to one of the most vital yet neglected teachings in the Bible. You see, Jesus is more than your Saviour on Calvary in the past and your coming King when He returns in the future. Right now, in heaven's sanctuary, He is serving as your personal Priest. He offers you the forgiveness, the comfort, the strength you need to rise above the past and fulfill your potential in the future.

It's certainly not an easy road back from suffering sexual abuse. But remember that your loving Lord is with you every step of the way. Linda's experience of recovery can be yours as well.

1. *The Jewish Encyclopedia* (New York: Funk and Wagnalls, 1904), s.v. "attorney."
2. W. M. Chandler, *The Trial of Jesus from a Lawyer's Standpoint* (Buffalo, N.Y.: W. S. Hein, 1983), vol. 1, pp. 153, 154.

Chapter 6

Overcoming Bankruptcy

Donald Trump. Celebrated dealmaker of the 1980s. High priest of glamor, wealth, and success.

Trump splashed his name throughout his magic kingdom. On the gleaming jets of the airline he bought. On his glittering hotels and golden casinos. On the most prestigious real estate in Manhattan. Even a bicycle race and a table game showcased the fame of his name.

Donald Trump became America's symbol of prosperity and security. His titanic empire seemed unsinkable.

Suddenly the unthinkable happened. Trump began plunging toward bankruptcy. Only emergency concessions by his creditors kept him afloat—at least temporarily.

The nightmare of bankruptcy. Could it ever happen to you?

In this chapter we'll discuss a simple safeguard to economic security, something overlooked by Donald Trump.

If anyone was secure from financial disaster, it was Donald Trump. Or so it seemed. In his bestselling book, *The Art of the Deal*, he trumpeted his remarkable rise to the heights of business success. Suddenly it all began to crumble. What happened?

To begin with, the real estate market took a turn for the worse, and other factors as well combined to threaten Trump's empire. Of course, Donald Trump isn't the only one in financial distress these days. Bankruptcy filings in the United States are mounting toward 900,000 a year.

Most American families live close to the jagged edge of bankruptcy—just a couple of paychecks away, in fact. If you are strung out on debt and short on savings, you may be a candidate to join the ranks of the homeless. Losing your job could put your family out on the streets faster than you might imagine.

Let me tell you about Bob and Judy and their nightmare with bankruptcy. It didn't have to happen to them. When they sped away from their wedding in their brand new Toyota, the world of opportunity lay open before them. Both were recent college graduates with good jobs in the field of medicine. And both liked to work hard.

Unfortunately, both Bob and Judy also enjoyed spending money. Lots of it. First came an apartment full of distinctive new furniture, followed by a lavish vacation. Why not—they deserved it all, didn't they? Within a year they ran up their charge cards to the limit. Then a beautiful new baby made an unscheduled appearance, placing an added strain on the family budget. As unexpected medical expenses multiplied, Bob and Judy found themselves buried beneath a blizzard of bills.

You can guess what happened next. The creditors came calling. Day and night they demanded their due. Collection agencies don't care about new babies and doctor bills—they just want their money—and they want it now. Finally, Bob and Judy decided there was only one way out. With a lot of guilt and regret, they filed for bankruptcy.

Listen, my friend. If you are spending more than you are earning, sooner or later judgment day will come for you as well.

It makes no difference whether you are Bob and Judy or anyone else—even Donald Trump.

Deeply concerned, Bob and Judy filed for chapter 13 of the United States Bankruptcy Code, which permitted them protection from creditors while they reorganized their finances. Their lawyer put them in touch with a qualified debt counselor, who taught them the importance of good, old-fashioned discipline in dealing with dollars.

The counselor had them fill out a daily spending log, something that might be good for all of us. Bob and Judy had to record every dollar expended from their next several paychecks so they could learn where the leaks might be in order to plug them. They were astonished to discover the many little ways that money was slipping through their fingers. It was tough medicine, but finally they learned to stop asking where the money went—and started telling it where to go.

As time went on, Bob and Judy got back on their feet. After a few years they even managed to clear their credit enough to get approval on a home loan. And bit by bit, they are determined to pay back every creditor.

Well, Bob and Judy's story has a happy ending. They overcame their bankruptcy. But they didn't have to put themselves through such trauma. In most cases, bankruptcy can be avoided. The most obvious prevention is to either increase income or decrease expenses.

Increasing income might mean overworking yourself and in the process ruining health and family life. I believe it's more prudent to discipline spending. That old saying can't be overworked: "A penny saved is a penny earned."

Another factor in maintaining solvency is good financial planning. Besides the obvious need to keep our family fed and housed, other goals deserve priority, such as getting out of debt. Eventually, perhaps owning a home. Saving for the education of children. Preparing for retirement.

Without question, escaping the trap of indebtedness should be near the top of our list. Interest expense on our debts is money down the drain—we can't even claim it as a tax deduction anymore.

Some advisors recommend avoiding all debt except for buying a house. That's preferable but perhaps not always possible—at times we may have no option except to purchase on credit. But except for a home mortgage and possibly a car, borrowing can open the door to trouble. You don't need me to lecture you about those convenient yet dangerous slivers of plastic we call credit cards. Many families have found it necessary to cut them up, burn them, or otherwise destroy them. Others can carry their MasterCard without using it except in an emergency.

An emergency, by the way, is only when there's a genuine need. Not when Radio Shack has a one-day special on stereos.

So I urge you to put your debts on a diet! You can't afford any extra burden on your paycheck—or your marriage!

We don't need to plunge into debt to invest in what lasts. Consider Mother Teresa. The whole world admires that dear soul for her self-sacrificing ministry to homeless sufferers on the streets of Calcutta. Only God knows how many children she has saved from starvation; eternity alone will tell how much good she has accomplished. Surely she is fulfilling her appointed role in ministering to the needs of others.

What about you and me? We may not be called overseas to do exactly what Mother Teresa does, but God has work for us as well. Whatever advantage we have—whether it be our finances, education, trade skills, or extra time available, perhaps—every blessing we have makes us the servant of those who lack. People helping people; that's the Bible way. Calling this "a thousand points of light" is simply a new name for an ancient and divinely ordained lifestyle.

John Wesley, founder of the Methodists, offered some sage counsel for financial planning: Earn all you can, then save all you can, so you can give all you can. Old-fashioned, rock-solid wisdom, wouldn't you say? Wesley knew nothing of the quick-fix lottery jackpot that millions today fruitlessly fantasize about.

There was another financial secret John Wesley had. This brings us to the heart of our spiritual responsibilities in dealing with our dollars—something not understood by the financial advisors of this world (Matthew 6:33): "Seek first the kingdom of God and His righteousness, and all these things shall be added to you."

Putting God first in our lives means putting Him first in our finances too—and doing so ensures our own stability. In other words, keeping God first keeps us first. Here's what the Bible says to do (Proverbs 3:9, 10): "Honor the Lord with your possessions, and with the firstfruits of all your increase; so your barns will be filled with plenty."

Have you noticed that God's call to financial commitment comes with His promise to take care of us? And on the other hand, the Bible also warns about the sad results of unfaithful stewardship.

Years ago, in one of the crowded cities of India, a speeding taxi struck a street urchin. A government official who witnessed the accident rushed the badly injured boy to a nearby hospital, where he gradually recovered.

Every day the official and his wife visited their young friend, becoming quite fond of him. Since he had no family, they decided to adopt him. Upon his release from the hospital, they joyfully brought him to their mansion as one of their own family.

Every day the mother brought her son back to the hospital to get his bandages changed. One morning she found herself especially busy and asked the boy if he could go by himself. "Of course," he replied proudly, "I know my way around this city." The mother gave him a dollar and a quarter to pay the doctor, and with a smile and a kiss, bade him farewell.

The boy set off for the hospital. Then, just as he turned the corner, a temptation crossed his mind. He stopped, opened his hand, and stared at the shining coins. Never before had he held so much money. Why did he have to give them to the doctor?

For a minute he stood there thinking. Then the decision was made. Clutching his coins, the boy raced down the street, never to be seen again.

The father he abandoned had considerable wealth. All his other children were university graduates who eventually held high positions in government and business. He planned to give his new son every advantage, even making him an heir to the family fortune. But the little fellow threw it all away—he threw his life away for one dollar and twenty-five cents.

How tragic! The greedy boy made a shortsighted investment. And we must beware of making the same mistake by investing in such things as illicit pleasure, alcohol, narcotics, and extravagant cars. When God instructs us to be faithful stewards, committing what we have to be used for His glory, He guarantees our deepest happiness.

What is God's plan for faithful stewardship? We find it here in the Bible (Malachi 3:10):

> "Bring all the tithes into the storehouse, that there may be food in My house, and prove Me now in this," says the Lord of Hosts, "if I will not open for you the windows of heaven and pour out for you such blessing that there will not be room enough to receive it."

The tithe, you may know, is 10 percent of our income, which God claims as His own. Some denounce tithe paying as a legalistic leftover from Moses on Mount Sinai. Actually, this common-sense principle of financial management can be traced to Abraham, the pioneer of our faith covenant with God.

In addition to tithe, the Bible speaks of offerings, too, as we are able to give. Is God expecting too much of us with our tithes and offerings? Not when we consider what He has done on our behalf. Our financial commitment to Him can only faintly reflect His gift to us in Christ.

Jesus, you recall, had been rich with the treasures of heaven. He enjoyed wealth we can't even imagine, yet He laid it all aside, coming to planet Earth as the poorest of the human family. And why did He live and die among us? So He could offer us a sound investment—lifelong security on earth followed by eternal riches in heaven.

How can we receive all that God offers us? First, we must declare bankruptcy. That's right—bankruptcy! We must confess that we are absolutely bankrupt of any worthiness or goodness in ourselves. Our only hope is in God's mercy, which comes to us through Jesus Christ. And there's more. We must also admit that we are bankrupt of any wisdom or strength to help ourselves. We must live by faith in God's guidance and power for daily living.

We've been discussing the spiritual aspects of our finances. The Bible says that God makes us "joint heirs with Christ." In other words, everything Jesus owns belongs to us too.

Do you realize that you are eternally rich in Christ? As rich as He is in everything? Of course, it may not seem that way right now—God knows that in this world of temptation we are better off without too many possessions to distract us. So He holds most of our wealth in trust until Jesus comes.

The humble disciples who followed Jesus when He walked this earth knew more about good financial management than most economists today. Notice this interesting conversation about investments that the apostle Peter had with Jesus (Mark 10:28-31):

> Peter began to say to Him, "See, we have left all and followed You." Jesus . . . said, "Assuredly, I say to you, there is no one who has left house or brothers or sisters or father or mother or wife or children or lands, for My sake and the gospel's, who shall not receive a hundredfold now in this time . . . with persecutions—and in the age to come, eternal life. But many who are first will be last, and the last first."

Did you catch that—a hundredfold return from our investment! This figures out to 10,000 percent interest accrued to us right now in this world. Not necessarily in the form of material wealth. Probably not, in fact. Rather, a wealth of God's lovingkindness, peace of mind, and the assurance of His salvation. Ten thousand percent interest right now, plus eternal life later.

Let's forget about the lottery jackpot—what do you say?

Here is something sure, something certain. I can't find any bankers or brokers who offer anything close to what God has guaranteed for our lives here and now—and beyond that, eternal life in heaven!

Let me tell you about a man who received incredible returns from his investments in the kingdom of God. Brother Andrew, they called him. Andrew's business was smuggling Bibles through what used to be Europe's Iron Curtain.

One day back in 1961, Brother Andrew loaded up his little old Volkswagen and headed east from Holland with his friend, Hans. As they wound their way through Germany's lush valleys and meadow lands, they prayed that the hidden Bibles they were carrying would safely find their way into the hands of Russian believers.

As they passed through Poland, their pulses picked up. Could they really slip their sacred cargo past the snarling guard dogs and bristling rifles of the Soviet border guards?

Yes! They made it through! With hallelujahs in their hearts, Andrew and Hans hurried on toward Moscow. Arriving at their destination, they located the Baptist church and showed up for Thursday-night prayer meeting.

Now they had to be really careful. Whom could they safely entrust with their smuggled treasure? They suspected that the KGB had informants in the audience—sometimes even pastors were under pressure to report Bible smugglers. Silently they prayed for guidance.

After the service, Brother Andrew and Hans lingered in the lobby, studying the faces of the 1,200 worshipers who were shuffling out the door. Suddenly they saw him—a thin, balding man in his forties.

"There's our man!" Hans whispered. Brother Andrew nodded.

Hearts thumping, they approached the stranger and cautiously introduced themselves. And what a surprise they got! This man had come all the way from Siberia in hopes of finding a Bible for his church. In fact, he had been instructed in a dream to make the long journey to Moscow.

At first, he hesitated—Bibles were scarce. But the dream had been authoritative. Without further delay, he obeyed.

After hearing the incredible story, Hans observed: "You were told to come westward for two thousand miles to get a Bible, and we were told to go eastward two thousand miles carrying Bibles. And here we are in Moscow tonight, recognizing each other the instant we meet."

The Siberian brother was excited—too excited, in fact. They had to calm him down quickly, lest he betray their glorious secret. Can you imagine the joy in his heart as, the next morning, he set off for home with a dozen precious Bibles?

In the next chapter you will read more thrilling stories about how God's people around the world have, through faith, overcome opposition of all kinds. Thank God that He has pierced the Iron Curtain. I've had the thrilling opportunity myself to travel freely from city to city conducting public crusades, proclaiming the gospel of Jesus Christ.

In Moscow, for example, thousands crowded one of the largest public halls as, night after night, I opened to them the Scriptures. Hundreds of men and women, young and old, discovered for themselves the reality of God and His love. Whatever the future may hold for them, they can face it confidently with peace of mind and hope for eternity. Yes, praise the Lord, after seven decades of spiritual bankruptcy, the Soviet people are recovering their spiritual heritage.

Have you discovered your own spiritual heritage? Have you declared personal bankruptcy regarding the counterfeit fulfillments of this world and accepted God's eternal riches in Christ Jesus? You can do so just now.

Chapter 7

Overcoming Opposition

Selma, Alabama. March 7, 1965. Bloody Sunday.

Under grim, overcast skies, 600 freedom marchers gathered for prayer outside Brown Chapel. Then they set off toward the state capital to campaign for their right to vote. As the solemn throng approached the muddy Alabama River, the look in their eyes showed commitment and determination.

Waiting on the other side of the bridge were their equally determined opponents, armed with bullhorns, clubs, and shotguns. Neither side backed down as the irresistible force of freedom confronted the immovable object of racism.

Suddenly the attack came. As the bruising blows of clubs descended and choking clouds of tear gas rose, anguished voices screamed, "Lord, have mercy!"

Opposition. It's always painful, especially when we are attacked for doing what is right. How do we overcome it? There's some vital information in store for you in this chapter about surviving the final conflict soon to burst upon our planet.

Thank God for the progress of freedom in America. Few of us have ever been attacked by tear gas and billy clubs, but we all know what it's like to encounter other forms of opposition. No matter how good a person you try to be, some people seem prejudiced against you. They just go out of their way to get in your way.

A work associate blocks the promotion or pay raise you earned. Your neighbor takes you to court over some trivial misunderstanding. Such is life in this world of sin.

We learn to expect opposition from people who don't like us. What's hard to handle is encountering opposition from people we really care about. Such as when you loan a friend some money out of compassion, and then he gossips about you behind your back. Or when you try to protect your teenagers from undue temptation, and all you get in return are grumbles and resentment.

Yes, opposition is especially difficult to accept when it comes by way of friends and family. It's particularly frustrating when these dear ones try to stop us from obeying the will of God. For example, in this book, we've discussed a number of exciting and vital teachings of the Bible. Some of what we studied might have been new to you, challenging a lifetime of cherished beliefs. You may have hesitated at first to obey the Lord, but then you decided to step out in faith no matter what the cost. "Everything will be fine now," you thought. "The Lord will bless my faithfulness." Then you discovered to your dismay that some of your loved ones misunderstood your new convictions. Perhaps they even placed themselves in opposition to your obedience. And now you wonder what to do.

Let me tell you about a new book that's full of insight and inspiration for overcoming opposition: *I Will Die Free*, the life story of Noble Alexander. I've never known of anyone in our time who faced more opposition yet endured so gracefully.

Noble lived in Cuba when the Communist revolution took over the country. Things have begun to change there lately, but for decades, believers in Cuba faced severe restrictions on their religious activities. The atheistic government might have left Noble alone had he kept his faith to himself. But the young layman felt compelled to obey Christ's command to share the gospel for lost souls to be saved. So they imprisoned him as a *plantado*—a rebel against the revolution.

Noble's ordeal began innocently enough. One evening the police pulled over his car and politely requested, "Would you mind coming with us to head-quarters? We'll only keep you five minutes."

Well, those five minutes turned out to be twenty-two years of incredible suffering. For forty-two days they subjected him to Chinese water torture, with broken glass under his heels. Then they starved him for six weeks, demanding that he renounce Jesus Christ. And after Noble refused to work on the Sabbath, they plunged him with his Adventist friends into a pool of raw sewage. Four weeks in a row these young men worshiped God, up to their chins in that slime, singing hymns of praise. Finally the guards realized that Noble and his friends were not going to surrender their Sabbath rest.

It would be impossible to describe all that Noble Alexander suffered during his two decades of imprisonment. Can you guess what was the worst torture he experienced? It was his beautiful young wife serving him notice of divorce and turning state's witness against him. Noble expected opposition from his enemies—but not from the one on earth he loved most.

How did he survive? He knew that his best friend of all, the Lord Jesus Christ, would never oppose him, never forsake him. Noble survived by faith in His promises.

Would you be interested to hear Noble's favorite promise—the Bible verse that anchored his faith during those dark decades in the dungeon? Here it is, from the book of Revelation (Revelation 2:10):

> Do not fear any of those things which you are about to suffer. Indeed, the devil is about to throw some of you into prison, that you may be tested, and you will have tribulation. . . . Be faithful until death, and I will give you the crown of life.

A thrilling message of hope. "Be faithful unto death," Jesus said, "and I will give you the crown of life."

God's faithful ones in that Cuban dungeon formed a secret prayer fellowship. Noble managed to arrange for a Bible to be smuggled in. Every night, Catholics, Baptists, Pentecostals, and Adventists prayed and sang together, united by their common faith in Christ.

Noble Alexander remained confined until 1984, when Jesse Jackson negotiated his release and deportation to the United States. Today he serves as a pastor for the Seventh-day Adventist Church in New England.

The complete story of Noble's persecution has just come out in a new book, *I Will Die Free*, available from the publishers of this book.

We've been discussing the challenge of overcoming opposition. Now let's look for solutions. To begin with, we must stop and think whether we brought the opposition upon ourselves by some mistake of our own. The Bible offers some important counsel (1 Peter 2:20, 21):

> What credit is it if, when you are beaten for your faults, you take it patiently? But when you do good and suffer for it, if you take it patiently, this is commendable before God. For to this you were called, because Christ also suffered for us,

leaving us an example, that you should follow
His steps.

When we suffer opposition, the first thing to do is
make sure we didn't bring some of it upon ourselves un-
necessarily. It's possible—even when trying to obey
God—that we haven't been as understanding and con-
siderate of others as we might be. Perhaps we aroused
their resistance by condemning them for not sharing our
convictions. Well, then we must apologize. The Lord
Jesus Christ, our great Example, showed tenderness toward those who opposed Him. Notice (1 Peter 2:23, 24):

> Who, when He was reviled, did not revile in
> return; when He suffered, He did not threaten,
> but committed Himself to Him who judges
> righteously; who Himself bore our sins in His
> own body on the tree, that we, having died to
> sins, might live for righteousness—by whose
> stripes you were healed. For you were like
> sheep going astray, but have now returned to
> the Shepherd and Overseer of your souls.

So Jesus didn't counterattack His opponents with
ridicule, and He didn't overwhelm them with threats.
Instead, He prayed for them and committed His cause
to the Father in heaven, the Judge who never makes
a mistake.

Our Lord is the only One who ever lived who never
deserved opposition. All the rest of us have strayed like
wandering sheep. But the Shepherd of our souls has
had mercy upon us, welcoming us home to His heart.
And now He expects us to share with fellow sinners the
same love and mercy that saves our souls (Romans
12:19, 21): "Do not take revenge, my friends, but leave
room for God's wrath, for it is written: 'It is mine to

avenge; I will repay,' says the Lord." "Do not be overcome by evil, but overcome evil with good" (NIV).

So there's the secret for overcoming opposition—
overcome evil by doing good! We don't do good to those
who oppose us because they deserve it; we love them
because God has loved *our* unworthy souls. Do you see
it? Our responsibility is to simply show the same
mercy that God bestows upon us.

I'm so glad I learned that I'm not the judge of all the
earth! Aren't you happy about that? God Himself will
deal with those who refuse to obey Him, those who
refuse to repent. Meanwhile, in this world of injustice
and hatred, let's make sure our own lives are right in
God's sight.

If we are prepared to meet the Lord in peace, the
second coming of our Lord Jesus Christ is our ultimate
deliverance from all opposition. And what a day it will
be when He bursts through the eastern sky!

What can we do to be ready? Notice the words of
Christ Himself in Matthew 7, verses 24 and 25:

Whoever hears these sayings of Mine, and
does them, I will liken him to a wise man who
built his house on the rock: and the rain descended, the floods came, and the winds blew
and beat on that house; and it did not fall, for
it was founded on the rock.

Tell me, my friend—are you founded upon the solid
rock of Jesus Christ? He is our sure foundation through
all the storms of life, through all the opposition we
must endure. Our Lord had a solemn warning for
those who neglect to obey Him (Matthew 7:26, 27):

Everyone who hears these sayings of Mine,
and does not do them, will be like a foolish man

who built his house on the sand: and the rain descended, the floods came, and the winds blew and beat on that house; and it fell. And great was its fall.

Many of you have been watching our "It Is Written" telecast for many years now. I so much appreciate your interest, your enthusiasm, your letters of support. You mean so much to me, more than you can know. I want you to be saved; I want you to overcome in the crisis so soon to burst upon our planet. So I must ask the question: Did you hear the warning in those verses we just read? A warning from Jesus especially for those who enjoy listening to the Word but neglect to act upon it—those who believe the truth but hesitate to obey it. Jesus said they are living on shifting sand. They will crumble during earth's final crisis.

No doubt about it—we must obey immediately when the Lord reveals truth to us from His Word. Think of it—it's not enough for passengers on a sinking ship to applaud the lifeboats—they must quickly move aboard. And it's not enough for you to appreciate the Word you hear week by week—you must act upon it. And the sooner the better for your soul. The final conflict of the ages is just upon us.

We must face reality—there will be hard times at the end of time. The Bible speaks of universal opposition ahead for God's faithful ones. That crowning jewel of Bible prophecy, the book of Revelation, predicts that just before Christ comes, all around the world, religious oppression will rear its ugly head. Finally a death sentence will be decreed for those whose faith in Christ leads them to honor all God's commandments. Listen to this (Revelation 12:17): "The dragon [that's the devil] was enraged with the woman [God's people, the church], and he went to make war with the rest of

her offspring [the remnant], who keep the commandments of God and have the testimony of Jesus Christ."

There we have it—God's faithful people will face the
ultimate opposition of the enemy in the soon-coming
conflict. I really do want you to be prepared, my friend.
The information you need to overcome the opposition
of earth's final crisis is in Revelation, the final book of
the Bible. You can get acquainted with its vital proph-
ecies in our book *The Rise and Fall of Antichrist*,
available from the publishers of this book.

Thank God, through whatever trouble lies ahead,
He has promised to preserve His people. Speaking of
Himself to His disciples, Jesus declared (Matthew
16:18, KJV): "Upon this rock I will build my church;
and the gates of hell shall not prevail against it."

Yes, nothing can ever destroy Christ's precious
church, though many through the ages have risen up
in opposition against it. First, the religious establish-
ment in Christ's own day persecuted the early disciples. Then the pagan Roman government. After
that, the church itself, fallen from grace, persecuted
its own members who refused to compromise their
faith. Here in the twentieth century, atheistic govern-
ments have waged war against God's people. And at
last will come that worldwide persecution. But God's
promise is sure—the gates of hell shall not prevail
against His people.

My friend Paul Harvey tells a story that's so incredible I could hardly believe it if I didn't know him so
well. A stack of sworn statements and legal documents
insists it really happened in a little town of North
Carolina, about one hundred years ago.

The Methodists of Swan Quarter decided to build
themselves a church. Unfortunately, the only lot they
could purchase was in a flood-endangered area on
Oyster Creek Road. They didn't want to build there.

Having no choice, however, they secured the deed to the land and went to work.

Soon their labor of love was finished, a small white structure propped up on brick pilings. On Sunday, September 16, 1876, they joyously dedicated the new house of God.

Three days later, a terrible storm burst upon the town. All night long and into the next day the wind raged while floodwaters rose. Finally, by Thursday afternoon, the storm had subsided. As the people of Swan Quarter ventured outside to survey the damage, an amazing sight met their eyes. The little white Methodist church was floating down Oyster Creek Road—drifting right on by! The floodwaters had gently lifted the entire structure and were ushering it slowly down the street.

The men of the town, once they recovered from their shock, grabbed coils of long rope and waded through the waist-deep water toward the white boat with a steeple. They managed to lash their ropes to the structure, but they couldn't stop it from moving onward.

Where in the world was it going?

Since all this happened more than a century ago, no one who saw it is alive today—but we do have comments from townspeople who have known members of the church who did see it happen. Here is testimony from Carolyn Harris:

"The tide came up, the building was washed off its blocks, and it started floating, and floated down this Oyster Creek Road, down to where it intersected the main street through Swan Quarter. It lodged against a great big frame store building. Then it was pushed off, so I'm told, and made a right turn. It floated down Main Street and landed on the site where the Methodists had wanted to build it in the first place."

But that's not all. Here's Paul Harvey's "rest of the story," as related by Tom Clarke, pastor of that same church today. The pastor stood in front of that same chapel as he finished the tale:

"The strange thing about this, was, of course, the way it floated here. Secondly, the people had sought to purchase this property and the owner refused to let them buy it. But he was so impressed by what had happened—he may even have been frightened—the hand of God so moved him that he donated this lot for the church building. And because the building had moved here so mysteriously, the people named this church "Providence"—moved by the hand of God—as if He had intended it to be here in the first place."

Well, evidently Someone up above, the ultimate landowner, had overruled human opposition to His purpose for that church.

And you know, He's doing the same today. In ways we cannot discern or even imagine, God is at work to fulfill His purpose for His people. A flood of opposition will try to sweep us away from our faithfulness during earth's final conflict, but our Lord's hand is at the helm. The enemies of God can only watch and wonder as His truth goes marching on.

It's happening already in the Soviet Union and Eastern Europe. It's happening in North and South America—Cuba too. It's going to happen in the lands of Islam, and yes, it will even happen in China. Praise the Lord—despite all human opposition, God's church is going through!

You can be on board, my friend. If you will entrust your life to Jesus day by day, He will keep you safe until that happy day, that wonderful day, that day of rejoicing, when He comes to take us home. God help us be ready for that day.